Paper Cranes

Paper Cranes

Dinah Dietrich

HEADMISTRESS PRESS

Copyright © 2015 by Dinah Dietrich.
All rights reserved.

ISBN-13: 978-0692585924
ISBN-10: 0692585923

This book may not be reproduced, in whole or in part, including illustrations, in any form (beyond that permitted by Sections 107 and 108 of the U.S. Copyright Law and except by reviewers for the public press), without written permission from the publishers.

Cover art by Marie Laurencin, *Le Bal élégant, La Danse à la campagne* (1913).
Cover & book design by Mary Meriam

PUBLISHER
Headmistress Press
60 Shipview Lane
Sequim, WA 98382
Telephone: 917-428-8312
Email: headmistresspress@gmail.com
Website: headmistresspress.blogspot.com

For Judith

Contents

Paper Cranes	1
Vortex	2
Dark Red Shoes	3
Queen of Anxiety	4
Kissing Poem 1	5
Kissing Poem 2	6
Dream Woman	7
Geraniums	8
Strange Food	9
For My Grandmother	10
Mother Drank	11
Coming Home 1972	12
Red Flowers	13
Retrospective	14
Water	15
Talking With My Father in a Restaurant	16
Brother	17
Grandma's Apron	18
Sleep	19
Wild Nights	20
Swimming in a Pond	21
Acknowledgments	23
About the Author	24

Paper Cranes

I remember the art class
when I was ten—
red paper birds—

once the teacher's daughter
took me upstairs
to her room—
touched me;
touched the beginning
breast bud
that was so tender

she was Japanese,
I did not know her name.
I thank her for giving me this gift,
the gift of the experience,
the gift of the memory.

I remember red paper cranes
that I constructed,
folding just so
until a form
began to emerge,

wings, a beak, a tail—
pull: oh, pull on the tail!
see the wings flap!

lots of paper birds
have flown
from my hands
like poems
into the sky of my life

Vortex

I'm so mad my hair could burst into flame
I look back
down the dark vortex that was life
that consumed me, swept me in
the blackness, a nightmare

that dark vortex
kept me for years
swirling

Now I close my eyes
see whirling blue sky
dizzy swirling blue

Now, healing
broken open like a geode
the starburst of joy
shimmers often.

Dark Red Shoes

I hurried all around
in dark red shoes,
ran around the campus
of the long-term hospital,
running on anxiety,
ran away from it
ran because of it.
Anxiety ran me.
But at least I wore clothes,
clean clothes.
The shoes were expensive,
my pink corduroy skirt
from a small exclusive shop.
Gone were the years of no baths
and unwashed hair.
Black depression, airless
as a closed coffin—
I could have died of it.
The dark night of life,
life near death, nothing less.
Soul eclipsed, I was chosen
to feel this pain.
Anita said, "This
is the winter of your life,"
she gave me the gift of hope.
I began to believe
that I could get better.
I lay in bed turned
toward closed shades—
sometimes small strips
of light leaked in
along the window edges.
The journey back was long
but I came back
slowly
slowly
into the light.

Queen of Anxiety

~ after J. Ruth Gendler's "Book of Qualities"

She's tall, stick skinny
wears a gold crown
wears bright red lipstick
applied thick, smeared.
Her hair, neon orange
stands on end.

She drinks
strong coffee all day;
she's a therapy junkie,
her forehead a wrinkled
field of worry.

She won her crown
through hard work:
from the energy
expended to just
survive.

She wonders
if there's anybody else
like her.
She longs
to find her tribe.

Kissing Poem 1

When I was young
I was surprised
when a young woman I knew
suddenly kissed me.

It was my first kiss,
shocking and marvelous
as the tender flower
that blossomed
between my legs.

Kissing Poem 2

When I was young, I kissed
my own shoulders.

Not knowing if this was normal,
I kept it secret.

Everything sexual
was hidden back then,

no one spoke of it.
I wondered

whether kissing my shoulders
was strange,

but since I was beautiful,
I would kiss myself again.

Dream Woman

I have devoted my life
to being a lesbian,
but almost never made love
with a woman.

I have met the woman
I always imagined.
She has short black hair—curly;
a round womanly body.

She undresses, reveals
a lavender bra, under that
her breasts are large,
splendid, with succulent nipples.

Her small hands
all over my body
like a blessing.

Geraniums

The red geranium petals
framed by spreading leaves,
blur against the window.
Beyond a door you sleep
slowed by summer heat.
Your breath is small.

Your rising breasts,
your hot, damp face
diminish
under loose brown hair.

When you wake we'll walk
outdoors through dizzy heat.

Strange Food

I remember
the night
I ate
Asian food
from
little
white cartons,
left over
from a restaurant
dinner.

A man
kissed me
in a room
full of plants.

I remember
his mouth

I remember
the room.

The food
from another
continent,

the intricate
taste.

For My Grandmother

You twisted your long hair
around your hands into a knot,

secured it with hair pins.

Your soft arms, your grey wool dress,
your red mouth kissing my cheek.

I liked to watch you dress.
You pulled on your pink corset,
dabbed red lipstick on your mouth.

I looked through bureau drawers:
the balls of rolled silk stockings,
long strands of fine white pearls.

Shoe bags hung on backs of doors
filled with high-heeled shoes.

You let me wear them to dress up.

A fine white line under my chin,
a scar from falling down stairs.

Mother Drank

She drinks more and more shots
from tiny glass cups,
royal blue. My mother
in a drunken rage
pulls down the beaded curtain.
Her rages are terrifying,
beyond control.

My mother, drunk,
slicing salad vegetables
cuts her thumb,
ignores the wound,
goes on
cutting vegetables
into the bowl.
Blood in the salad.

Coming Home 1972

Plants wait on my desk.
The furniture has been tagged with my name.
The thirty-three notebooks of my life
in a wooden box.

I take each fish from the water
put it in a small white carton
for the car trip.

My father arrives. We pack the car
and start for home. The fish in their boxes
seem too warm. I sprinkle water on the cartons.

Father, why did you leave me so long ago?
You didn't come home until the birth
of my brother.

I breathe in cigarette smoke. The fish want
their familiar water.

In my room at home,
I struggle for light.
The plants strangle
at the small window.

The fish
hover behind a rock,
eat as though starved.

My mother's long-ago voice
comes to me—gentle,
sad, loving.

My father's laugh
his red hair and business suit
bushy eyebrows and shirt from the laundry
intrude.

I listen to the radio.

Red Flowers

Mother planted bright red flowers
in her garden—
hummingbirds came,
their bright wings
beating fast, a blur
of wings—hovering

Mother told me
how she gave birth
how she watched in a mirror
until pain produced me finally
pushing me out
from that dark place
between her thighs

Retrospective

The red beet juice
stains the corn.

There is a dark-red leaf
in the tuna salad.

A Greek dressing
of yogurt and dill.

At the dinner table,
my mother is drunk.

Her face goes white & blank,
she stares.

My father says
he does not like
the leaf in the salad,

or the dill & yogurt.

After dinner,
I think of frightening things.

The crippled woman, I kissed
her cheek at a party.

I remember Mrs. Lusher,
her breasts poked through her dress.
She taught me to play the piano.

At the Museum of Modern Art,
in the cafeteria,
the pink blood came.

The beet juice
in the sink
turns watery, opaque.

Water

I cup my hands together,
drink the cold water
that runs into my hands
from the tap on the sink

I stand in the hospital bathroom,
and drink,
imagining
the small stream of fresh water
that flowed once,
in the Adirondacks,
upstate New York

my mother taught me
how to cup my hands and drink,
imagining she could teach me
how stones can flavor water

Talking With My Father in a Restaurant

I go swimming in my turquoise bathing suit.
Under water, I think I won't come up,
could hold my breath forever, my hair
floating behind me.

My father takes pictures, walks
to get batteries for his camera.
His hair is red.

He gives me money, and kisses my cheek.

Father, you left me as a child,
came back late
from the Navy.

Now you give me money,
and kiss my cheek.

We talk over hamburgers and french fries.
I tell you I live better, better.

Your blazing hair turns slowly white.

Your wide head and glasses.

You buy me clothes.
You give me your old white bathrobe.

You begin to notice my eyes.

Brother

A friend gives me a ride.
The night flows by the windows,
effortlessly dark, recalling
the warmth of soft wool blankets,
moving pictures behind closed eyes.

My brother is sleeping
in the seat beside me.
his jaw relaxes. His face
drifts into childhood.

My dolls got sick and vomited
while he built forts.

I cut my hair and wore Kotex
while he shot his friends
with his plastic forty-five.

I could still run my fingers
through the soft brush of his hair.

Grandma's Apron

As I walk past the mirror,
suddenly I see myself
in motion.
My apron of fat hangs down,
jiggles as I walk.

It's my big belly.
Suddenly, I am my grandmother.

She was big like me.
I loved her,
wrapped my arms around her tight
hug tight, hold tighter.
She squeezed back,
a true connection.

She said, "Grandma loves you, honey."
Her love was pure.

She fed me, cooked a lot,
baked me lemon-meringue pie
from scratch.

She loved me simply
in a way no one else could.

"I've got love in my tummy,"
the song said.

Once I made an apron
for Grandma.
Mother sewed:
apron strings so long
Grandma cried.

Sleep

Lying in bed,
I listen for sounds in the night.
Then my face closes;
voices drift through my head.
Without my knowing,
my shallow breath rises and falls.
I am not harmed in my sleep.
I do not struggle in dreams.
With my hands crossed over my chest,
there is no end to falling.
In my dreams I have no destination.
My face is closed.
How far could I walk without waking?

Wild Nights

When you want to write
first make strong coffee.

Every day of my life
holds strong poems
and strong coffee.

I am wild at night
in my apartment
making peanut butter toast,
making a poem.

The poem is harder to make
than the toast,
but both are luscious.

Swimming in a Pond

I undress near the car,
throw my clothes on the seat,
wade slowly into the water.

I sink back, surrender to floating.
My legs do scissor kicks.
Across the pond: blue sky, trees, red barns.
Those simple things.

Light floods the water.
A piece of green glass
glitters near my feet.

Water laps against my skin.
I move smoothly under the water.
Wordlessly I inhabit my body.

I think of the time I stayed indoors
lying in the dark,
my only light the knife-like strips
between window and shade.

Acknowledgments

Thanks to Judith Prest, who is birthing my writing. My words are ready to fly out into the world.

Thanks to Lynne Davidson, who has always taken an interest in my writing and cheered me on.

Thanks also to: Linda Sanchez, who showed me the world again after a fallow time. We had fun riding in the big red car. Tracy Jones, a helper through thick and thin. Betty Rutland, who has been like a second mother to me. Ellen Hiscox, for her interest in my writing. Esther Willison, who always shows up on birthdays—and whose daughter was a poet I shall miss always.

Thanks to all the people, too numerous to mention individually, who have sparked my imagination and fed my interest in poetry over the years.

Thanks to the editors of the following publications where these poems first appeared:

A Slant of Light: Contemporary Women Writers of the Hudson Valley: "Red Flowers"

elephantjournal: "Kissing Poem 1," "Kissing Poem 2"

Sinister Wisdom: "Vortex"

The Third Berkshire Anthology: A Collection of Literature & Art: "Geraniums," "For My Grandmother"

About the Author

Dinah Dietrich lives and writes in Schenectady, New York. She has a BA in Creative Writing from Bennington College, and an MA in Literature from the University of Massachusetts, Amherst. She has always been a voracious reader of women authors and lesbian literature. She loves the poetry of Elizabeth Bishop, Adrienne Rich, and Mary Oliver.

Headmistress Press Books

Lovely - Lesléa Newman
Teeth & Teeth - Robin Reagler
How Distant the City - Freesia McKee
Shopgirls - Marissa Higgins
Riddle - Diane Fortney
When She Woke She Was an Open Field - Hilary Brown
God With Us - Amy Lauren
A Crown of Violets - Renée Vivien tr. Samantha Pious
Fireworks in the Graveyard - Joy Ladin
Social Dance - Carolyn Boll
The Force of Gratitude - Janice Gould
Spine - Sarah Caulfield
Diatribe from the Library - Farrell Greenwald Brenner
Blind Girl Grunt - Constance Merritt
Acid and Tender - Jen Rouse
Beautiful Machinery - Wendy DeGroat
Odd Mercy - Gail Thomas
The Great Scissor Hunt - Jessica K. Hylton
A Bracelet of Honeybees - Lynn Strongin
Whirlwind @ Lesbos - Risa Denenberg
The Body's Alphabet - Ann Tweedy
First name Barbie last name Doll - Maureen Bocka
Heaven to Me - Abe Louise Young
Sticky - Carter Steinmann
Tiger Laughs When You Push - Ruth Lehrer
Night Ringing - Laura Foley
Paper Cranes - Dinah Dietrich
On Loving a Saudi Girl - Carina Yun
The Burn Poems - Lynn Strongin
I Carry My Mother - Lesléa Newman
Distant Music - Joan Annsfire
The Awful Suicidal Swans - Flower Conroy
Joy Street - Laura Foley
Chiaroscuro Kisses - G.L. Morrison
The Lillian Trilogy - Mary Meriam
Lady of the Moon - Amy Lowell, Lillian Faderman, Mary Meriam
Irresistible Sonnets - ed. Mary Meriam
Lavender Review - ed. Mary Meriam

www.ingramcontent.com/pod-product-compliance
Lightning Source LLC
Chambersburg PA
CBHW070048070426
42449CB00012BA/3190